My Farm

My Goats

By Heather Miller

Children's Press
A Division of Grolier Publishing
New York / London / Hong Kong / Sydney
Danbury, Connecticut

Special thanks to the Hanner family and for the use of their farm, Elainewood Acres

Photo Credits: All photos by Thaddeus Harden

Contributing Editor: Jennifer Ceaser
Book Design: MaryJane Wojciechowski

Visit Children's Press on the Internet at:
http://publishing.grolier.com

Library of Congress Cataloging-in-Publication Data

Miller, Heather.
  My goats / by Heather Miller.
    p. cm. — (My farm)
  Includes bibliographical references (and index).
  Summary: A young boy describes how he cares for the goats living on his farm.
  ISBN 0-516-23107-3 (lib. bdg.) — ISBN 0-516-23032-8 (pbk.)
  1. Goats—Juvenile literature. [1. Goats.] I. Title.

SF383.35.M53 2000
636.3'9—dc21

                                             00-024384

Contents

Hello, I'm Roberto.

Would you like to meet my kids?

5

Yes, I have kids!

A baby goat is a **kid**.

My kids are named Gigi and George.

This is their mother, Lily.

A mother goat is a **doe.**

9

This is their father, Art.

A father goat is a **buck**.

You can tell that Art is a buck.

A buck has a long **beard**.

13

I feed my goats hay.

I also feed them **alfalfa**.

Alfalfa is a special kind of hay.

15

A kid needs its mother's milk to grow strong.

I feed my kid the milk from a **bottle**.

I need milk to grow strong, too!

My doe gives us milk.

Only a doe can give milk.

19

At night, my goats stay in the **barn**.

Goodnight, my goats!

New Words

alfalfa (al-**fal**-fah) a special kind of hay

barn (**barn**) a place where farm animals stay at night

beard (**beerd**) hair or fur on the chin

bottle (**bot**-l) something that holds milk so that it can be fed to a baby

buck (**buk**) a father goat

doe (**doh**) a mother goat

kid (**kid**) a baby goat

To Find Out More

Books

Billy Whiskers: The Autobiography of a Goat
by Francis Trego
Dover Publications

Mountain Goats
by Frank J. Staubby
The Lerner Publishing Group

The Hungry Billy Goat
by Rita Milios
Children's Press

Web Sites

Animaldoc.com
http://lam.vet.uga.edu/kids/goats/default.html
This site has a lot of information about goats. Look at goat pictures and learn fun facts about goats!

Kids Farm
http://www.kidsfarm.com
Learn all about different kinds of farm animals, including goats.

Index

alfalfa, 14   doe, 8, 18   milk, 16, 18

barn, 20   hay, 14

beard, 12

bottle, 16   kid, 6, 16

buck, 10, 12

About the Author

Heather Miller lives in Cambridge, Massachusetts, with her son, Jasper. She is a graduate student at Harvard University.

Reading Consultants

Kris Flynn, Coordinator, Small School District Literacy, The San Diego County Office of Education

Shelly Forys, Certified Reading Recovery Specialist, W.J. Zahnow Elementary School, Waterloo, IL

Peggy McNamara, Professor, Bank Street College of Education, Reading and Literacy Program

24